Different Places, Different Faces

Contents

Features

What do a mosquito net and the rain forest canopy have in common? You'll find out on page 8.

Is that a walking leaf? Turn to page 12 for fast facts on the antics of leaf-cutter ants and their work in the Amazon rain forest.

The jungle jaguar is hungry. Will she find dinner tonight? Turn to **The Jaguar** on page 16 for more on this mighty predator.

Have you ever heard of a sing-sing? **Visit a Sing-Sing** on page 24 will give you travel tips and the inside story on this special celebration.

What different foods do snakes eat?

Visit **www.rigbyinfoquest.com** for more about **SNAKES**.

Different Places

Many places around the world are hot and wet. There is no spring, summer, autumn, or winter. There are only two seasons—a hot, wet season and a warm, drier season. These places are called **tropical.** Here, even the drier season is often wet! Rainfall may be more than 20 feet a year. That's a lot of rain!

Plants grow well in these hot, wet places. Much of the land is covered in thick rain forest, or jungle.

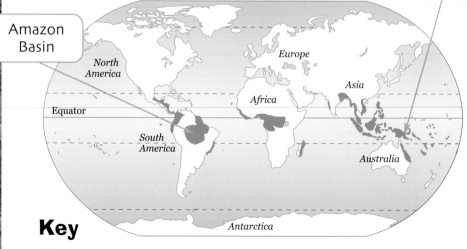

Papua New Guinea

Amazon Basin

North America

Europe

Asia

Africa

Equator

South America

Australia

Antarctica

Key

Tropical rain forests of the world

4

The tropical rain forests of the world provide homes for more than half the life-forms on Earth. Many rain forests are endangered because people clear the trees for timber and farmland.

Tropical Rain Forests

Tropical rain forests have four different layers of plant growth. These are:

- the forest floor
- the **understory**
- the **canopy**
- the **pavilion**

In each layer, there are many different plants and animals. Special features help them survive at the level where they live. Many of the plants and animals that live in the rain forest are found nowhere else on Earth. To help save them, some countries set aside parts of rain forests as reserves.

Key to Animals

1. Harpy eagle	16. Lizard
2. Howler monkeys	17. Coati
3. Pygmy anteater	18. Ocelot
4. Kinkajou	19. Quetzal
5. Sloth	20. Tapir
6. Spider monkey	21. Bat
7. Tree porcupine	22. Fowl
8. Toucans	23. Anaconda
9. Zebra butterfly	24. Caiman
10. Hummingbird	25. Snake
11. Tree boa	26. Capybara
12. Tree anteater	27. Poison arrow fro
13. Tree frog	28. Armadillo
14. Scarlet macaws	29. Bird-eating spid
15. Jaguar	30. Hoatzin

The pavilion

The canopy

The understory

The forest floor

The Rain Forest Floor

The rain forest floor is damp and dark.
The plants that grow there often
have large leaves to catch the light.
Many seedlings can only sprout when
a big tree falls. The seedlings then
grow fast and tall toward the light.

Termites eat
bark, wood,
and dead plants.

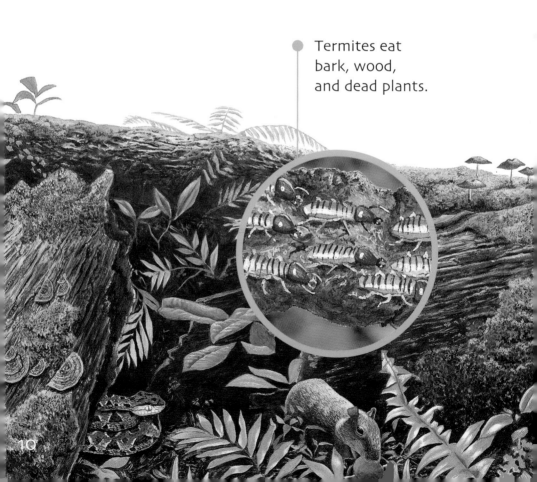

The jaguar is the main meat eater of the South American rain forest.

Snails are plant eaters. They get their food from plants. When the snails are eaten, they then provide food for meat eaters such as frogs and birds.

Dead or Alive?

This tree is dead, but it is "alive" with activity. Mosses, seedlings, and fungi grow on it. Insects make homes in it. Animals feed on the bark and the insects that live there. In the hot, wet environment, this fallen tree will soon disappear and new plants will fill the space.

Rain Forest Life

A tropical rain forest is home to more plants and animals than any other place on Earth. Some trees grow as tall as 20-story buildings. They rise above the canopy, which lets in very little light. To get some light, plants called **epiphytes** grow on the trunks and branches of the tall trees. Vines climb up the trees toward the light.

WORD BUILDER

A *canopy* is a covering. It comes from the Greek word *konopeion*, which means "mosquito net."

The Amazon Basin

From the air, the Amazon Basin looks like an ocean of green. It is the world's largest area of tropical rain forest. Scientists think that there may be as many as 100 kinds of trees in every acre of this forest. They think more than 1,500 kinds of birds may live in these trees.

The rain forest echoes with the calls of frogs, insects, birds, and mammals. It squeaks, sputters, howls, and whistles all day and all night.

Red-eyed tree frog

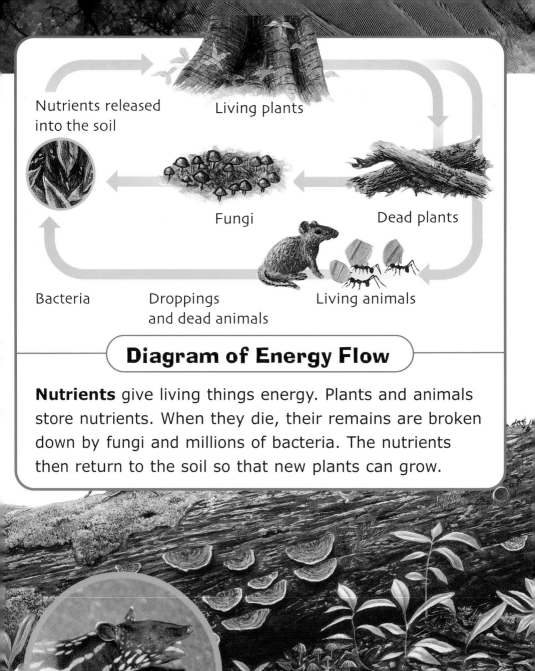

Nutrients released into the soil

Living plants

Fungi

Dead plants

Bacteria

Droppings and dead animals

Living animals

Diagram of Energy Flow

Nutrients give living things energy. Plants and animals store nutrients. When they die, their remains are broken down by fungi and millions of bacteria. The nutrients then return to the soil so that new plants can grow.

Tapirs wander the rain forest floor looking for a meal of leaves and fruit.

Tree frogs climb from tree to tree to catch insects.

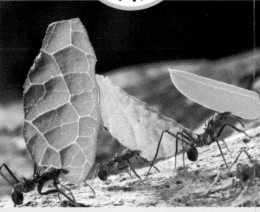

Leaf-cutter ants snip off pieces of leaves for their nest. Back in the nest, they chew the pieces into "compost." This helps fungus to grow. Leaf-cutter ants eat fungus.

Spot the Snake

Rain forests are home to many kinds of snakes. The vine snake grows to 7 feet long, but its body is no more than half an inch around. It eats small birds.

What different foods do snakes eat?
Visit **www.rigbyinfoquest.com** for more about **SNAKES.**

SITESEEING
• PLANTS & ANIMALS •

Hyacinth macaw

Cottontop tamarin

The Jagua

It is getting dark. On the forest floor, a piglike peccary is looking for food. A female jaguar slinks after it. In a safe hideaway under a fallen tree, her two hungry cubs are waiting to be fed.

The jaguar is not a strong runner. She must stalk her prey quietly and slowly until she can pounce on it. The peccary looks up. The jaguar flattens herself on the ground. The peccary begins to eat. The jaguar bursts from hiding and kills the peccary with a blow from her powerful paws and a bite to its neck. It's dinnertime!

Peccary

Jaguar

Don't Be Fooled

Jaguars are bigger than leopards. They also have small spots inside larger spots. Leopards do not.

Leopard

A jaguar scratches to mark its territory.

Jaguars face many dangers, but the greatest danger comes from people. The tropical rain forests where jaguars live are cut for timber and for farmland. Although jaguars are protected, people still hunt them for their beautiful coats. Jaguars need greater protection if they are to survive.

Cheetahs have tear marks below their eyes.

Cheetah

People of the Amazon

People have lived in the Amazon rain forest of South America for many thousands of years. Once, millions of people lived there. Today, only about 250,000 people live in the rain forest.

These people live in small groups. They know how to use the plants and animals of the rain forest for food, medicine, and for hunting. They grow vegetables in small, cleared spaces in the jungle and cook their food in the same way their people did long ago.

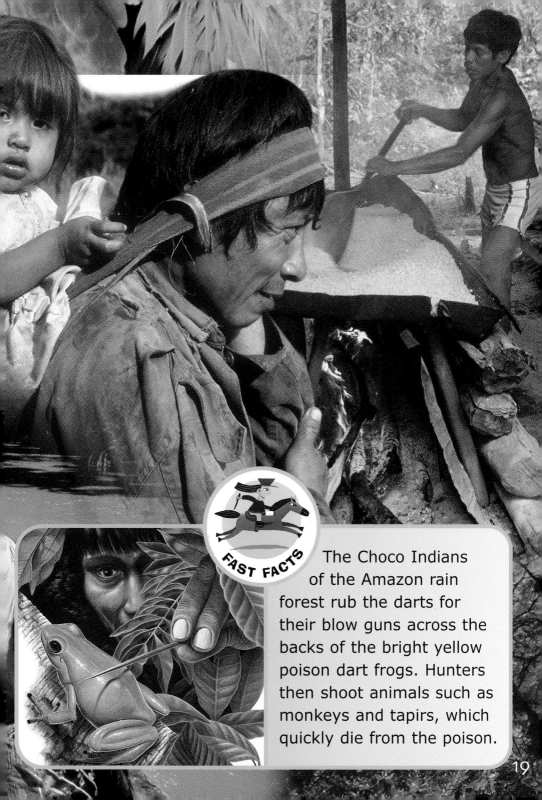

FAST FACTS

The Choco Indians of the Amazon rain forest rub the darts for their blow guns across the backs of the bright yellow poison dart frogs. Hunters then shoot animals such as monkeys and tapirs, which quickly die from the poison.

19

Papua New Guinea

The islands of Papua New Guinea lie far away from the Amazon Basin. These islands are wild, mountainous, and almost fully covered in thick rain forest.

Many strange and beautiful plants and animals are found in Papua New Guinea. They are not endangered, because people do not often cut down trees in this steep, rugged land.

Cassowary with chicks

Spotted cuscus

Tree pythons

21

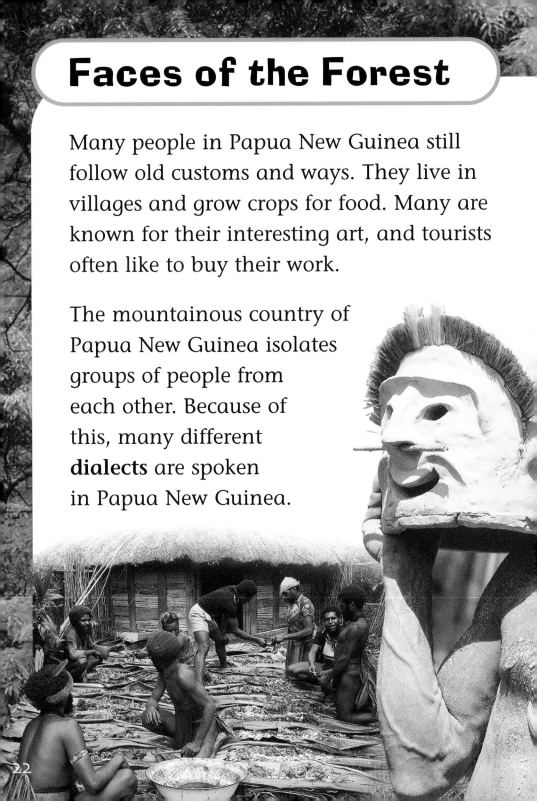

Faces of the Forest

Many people in Papua New Guinea still follow old customs and ways. They live in villages and grow crops for food. Many are known for their interesting art, and tourists often like to buy their work.

The mountainous country of Papua New Guinea isolates groups of people from each other. Because of this, many different **dialects** are spoken in Papua New Guinea.

People have lived in Papua New Guinea for about 50,000 years. Some still build their homes using traditional methods and materials.

23

IN FOCUS

Visit a Sing-Sing

Tourists can experience a festival of singing, dancing, and feasting in the misty highlands of Papua New Guinea. Here, people enjoy sing-sing celebrations that were once hidden in this land of boiling volcanoes, tropical jungles, steamy swamps, and winding rivers.

Thousands of brightly painted Wigmen warriors gather each July for the famous Highland Show sing-sing. Their faces are brilliantly painted and their headdresses woven with flowers and feathers. The warriors chant, stomp, and dance to the beat of many drums. The sing-sing is an experience few visitors ever forget.

Travel Tips

Getting there:
• You'll need a passport and a visa.

Touchdown:
• You'll land at Port Moresby International Airport, Papua New Guinea.

Getting around:
• Use a small plane, rental car, boat, or canoe.

Where to stay:
• Stay at lodges along the Highlands Highway.

Weather:
• It's hot, sticky, and rainy all year!

HOT TIP
Bring lots of insect repellent. The bugs BITE!

Glossary

canopy – the thick layer of leaves and branches formed by the very tall trees in a forest

dialect – the special words and way of speaking used by people in a certain area. Dialects form when groups of people live far away from other groups of people.

epiphyte – (*EHP uh fyt*) a plant that grows on another plant. Many epiphytes provide food for small animals.

nutrients – any substance that is needed for the life and growth of plants and animals. Minerals and vitamins are nutrients.

pavilion – the very top layer of a forest. Trees that form the pavilion are able to grow even taller than canopy trees.

tropical – a word that describes what it is like in places that are in the Tropics. The Tropics are not far from the Equator. Tropical places are hot and wet.

understory – the lower layer of plants in a forest. The plants that form the understory do not grow very tall.

Index

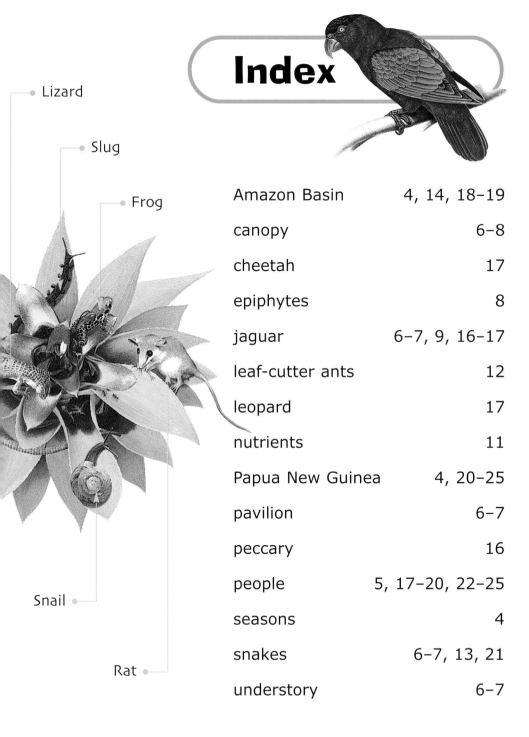

Lizard

Slug

Frog

Snail

Rat

Discussion Starters

1 People are clearing huge areas of the world's rain forests every day for timber and farmland. What effects might this have on all of Earth's living things?

2 Rain forests are full of wonderful surprises. New kinds of plants and animals are often discovered there. Even though you might live far from a rain forest, what can you do to help protect rain forest plants and animals?

3 If you could dance at a sing-sing, what sort of headdress would you design? How would you paint your face?